YOUR KNOWLEDGE HAS VALUE

- We will publish your bachelor's and master's thesis, essays and papers

- Your own eBook and book - sold worldwide in all relevant shops

- Earn money with each sale

Upload your text at www.GRIN.com and publish for free

Bibliographic information published by the German National Library:

The German National Library lists this publication in the National Bibliography; detailed bibliographic data are available on the Internet at http://dnb.dnb.de .

This book is copyright material and must not be copied, reproduced, transferred, distributed, leased, licensed or publicly performed or used in any way except as specifically permitted in writing by the publishers, as allowed under the terms and conditions under which it was purchased or as strictly permitted by applicable copyright law. Any unauthorized distribution or use of this text may be a direct infringement of the author s and publisher s rights and those responsible may be liable in law accordingly.

Imprint:

Copyright © 2018 GRIN Verlag
Print and binding: Books on Demand GmbH, Norderstedt Germany
ISBN: 9783668697300

This book at GRIN:

https://www.grin.com/document/424294

Edward Wolber-Wood

Online Learning. Value, Viability, and Cultural Impact

GRIN Verlag

GRIN - Your knowledge has value

Since its foundation in 1998, GRIN has specialized in publishing academic texts by students, college teachers and other academics as e-book and printed book. The website www.grin.com is an ideal platform for presenting term papers, final papers, scientific essays, dissertations and specialist books.

Visit us on the internet:

http://www.grin.com/

http://www.facebook.com/grincom

http://www.twitter.com/grin_com

Edward Wolber-Wood
Spring 2018

Online Learning: Value, Viability, and Cultural Impact

A Few Words From The Author

We are living in the gilded age of learning. This is something that we take for granted constantly; gone are the days of barroom arguments on who won the American League MVP award in 1995, the Academy Award for best picture in 2008, or whether French Fries were actually invented in France (they were not). We have supercomputers in our pockets that possess the entirety of human knowledge and can access it in microseconds with a few taps of the finger or a "Hey Siri". The proliferation of the information superhighway has ushered in a new culture of teaching and learning. Do you want to learn how to poach an egg? Skin a buck? Run a regression analysis? Not only can you find articles, videos, step-by-step instruction pages, and blogs relating to anything you could possibly think to want to learn, but information technology has come so far that you do not even need to finish typing what you want to learn into Google before predictive search AI can finish your thought for you. With all of this information so readily available, why is it that there has been a historically pessimistic view of accredited degrees, certifications, and continued professional education being delivered via the internet? Throughout this paper, I will be outlining the value of an online education when compared apples-to-apples with a Brick and Mortar-earned degree, the viability of online learning as we progress further into the 21st century, and the cultural impact and perception of online learning. Through pragmatic data analysis, objective explanation of both sides of the issue, and my experience as a student who has spent years at a Four-Year Institution of Higher Learning, living on campus, joining Student Government and Greek Life, and participating in the traditional "college experience", as well as years working full-time while taking courses here at Arizona

State via distance education. While I align myself firmly with the school of thought that distance education is the future of learning, I will do my best as a researcher to analyze the data for statistical significance and see beyond the rhetoric of both sides of the issue.

Distance Learning: A Look Back

At the beginning of the 20th Century, much like the spread of the internet that we saw 100 years later, a new communication network was emerging: the modern postal system. Colleges in the early 1900's saw the utility of such a service straightaway and began to spread their education far beyond the reach of a traditional lecture hall or classroom by distributing courses through the postal system so that anyone with a mailing address could enroll in college courses. These correspondence courses enabled people who would otherwise never be able to attain higher education the ability to do so, as esteemed UW Professor Fredrick Jackson Turner said, "the machinery of distance learning would carry irrigating streams of education into the arid regions of the country". Not long after its introduction, postal courses had four times as many enrollees as every University in the Nation combined. Broader access was not the only benefit that its early proponents voiced, also maintaining that tests and assignments could be specifically tailored to each student and allowed for an "intimate tutorial relationship" with the professors in favor of the crammed-full classrooms of typical American colleges. Nearly one-hundred years later, we are seeing many of those claims articulated anew in support of Online Learning. The proliferation of online learning has made it possible for those who cannot attend college for any number of reasons a chance to better themselves and their futures. As William Bennet, Former United States Education Secretary stated, there is an Athens-like Renaissance in the making in the form of online learning. Now, the long-engrained barriers that kept many from achieving higher education have been eliminated due to the ability for courses to be taken online. In 2002, the number of students that took at least one online course from an accredited university was 1.6 million - that number in 2016 was over 6 million. As of 2018, there are 28,249 online degree and certificate programs available that are accredited by agencies recognized by the United States Department of Education.

Online Education's Relevance in 2018: Culturally and Economically

With the ability to access the entirety of human knowledge at our fingertips has come an inherent distrust of what we hear in person. Years ago, prior to the advent of the smartphone, skepticism to a statement made by another was met with offense. Now, it is a foregone conclusion that any spewing of statistics or facts will be met with a quick internet-search to corroborate. We trust the internet more than we trust each other, and for good reason. In like fashion, my years of college experience have taught me that even our Professors may skew the facts and the data in their favor, not to mention in many courses where there is little useful data or the course is reliant on rhetoric and conjecture rather than pragmatism. The interesting thing about our trust in the internet over our fellow humans is that it does not carry over when talking about Higher-Education. As I am sure many of you have, I have often faced recourse, skepticism, and even admonishment when I have informed other that I take online courses. While the culture is shifting, many people, professors included, ascertain that online education is not "real school", that it could never take the place of an in-class education, or that its proliferation will lead to a gap between so-called elite-schools who use their professors and clout to take away from smaller or less-recognized universities ability to keep their classes full.

My first issue with the idea that online education is not as valuable as an in-class education comes from my experience in both environments. In my honors political theory course that I took in-class at the University of Houston, there were over 50 students in a lecture hall. This course was unique in that no lectures were given in class, but rather all of the readings and research was to be conducted prior to the class so that the lecture time could be spent engaging in debate, discussion, and deconstruction through conversation regarding what we were learning. I loved the class because I am an outgoing, boisterous, and charismatic person who enjoys being the center of attention and has never struggled with public speaking. However, of those fifty students, I shared those traits with 8-10 of them. Shyness, disdain for public speaking, self-doubt or fear of being made to look silly, resulted in the majority of the class only speaking up when motioned to do so by the instructor. On the contrary, when taking the online courses that I have here at ASU, every single student has the time to dedicate to articulating their own opinions at their own pace without the fear of speaking to a room full of strangers or being too shy to speak up. By allowing students to communicate online, we are allowing discourse and debate to occur amongst all students, not just those who are willing to speak up in class. This assessment pairs nicely with the fact that online education allows those who could otherwise never attend college in-class to do so. Whether it be that they are raising a family, working full-time, or fighting for our Country overseas, online education has allowed for them to continue to learn while balancing other aspects of their life. We are in an age of instant gratification and overstimulation. Boredom is obsolete. Think about all of those who had to refrain from college because they needed to provide for themselves or their family over the course of our history- those days are over.

While the traditional campus experience cannot be ignored, through analyzing the data, it is often overstated. The United States Department of Education found in its 2010 Technical Report "Evaluation of Evidence-Based Practices in Online Learning: a meta-analysis and Review of Online Learning Studies" found in their systematic analysis of research literature that students in online-learning conditions performed modestly better than those receiving face-to-face instruction. This data proved to be statistically significant, and the variables causing the gap showed to be additional learning time and instructional elements not received by students in control conditions. I maintain that the years I spent on campus, living at my fraternity house and attending sporting events, student government meetings, and basking in the "traditional college experience" were the most fun years of my life. However, did those things actually help me learn? I do not believe so. The cultural perception of online universities has already begun to shift, with the number of firms that use the recruiting site Insperity to find employees hiring a higher proportion of online-degree possessing potential employees rising year-over-year. A spokesperson from a Fortune 100 company stated that someone attaining an online education despite other priorities in their life shows a tenacity and grit that extends beyond the educational side of higher education and shows a propensity for time-management and hard work.

The other side of the coin are the economics of higher education. Tuition increases have far outpaced inflation rates for the last few decades, and there is no sign of that changing any time soon. In the United States Department of Education Office of Education Technology's "Understanding the Implications of Online Learning for Educational Productivity", Dr. Marianne Bakia from the University of Chicago assessed the potential cost-savings of online learning programs in comparison with face-to-face instruction and found consistent savings with online learning. I have included an exhibit from the paper that provides estimates for per-student spending in distance-education and on-campus from six different studies, of which all data was verified by an external auditor and proved to be statistically significant.

Exhibit 2: Comparison of Per-Pupil Spending

	Face-to-Face	Online
Wisconsin (Stuiber et al. 2010)	$11,397	$6,077
Utah (Sloan and Mackey 2009)	$5,683	$2,500
Survey of 14 States (Cavanaugh 2009a)	$9,138	$4,310
Florida (Florida Tax Watch 2007)	$6,291	$5,243
Ohio (Watson 2007)	$7,452	$5,383
Colorado (Watson 2004)	$8,917	$7,210

A recent report estimated the average per pupil costs of various models of online learning (Battaglino, T.M., M. Haldeman, and E. Laurans (2012). *The Costs of Online Learning*. Washington, DC: The Thomas B. Fordham Institute.) and found that virtual schools are likely to cost less than blended models. Based on expert opinion, the report found that the average per pupil cost of virtual schools ranged from $5,100 and $7,700, and the average per pupil cost of blended school models cost between $7,600 and $10,200.

The Future Of Online Learning: Viability, Thoughts, and Final Remarks

The Babson Survey Research Group's February 2018 report on Tracking Distance Education in the United States found that 71% of the degree granting institutions in the United

States participate in Online Education. While this notable proliferation blatantly exhibits long-term viability for Online Education, there are notable challenges that will need to be addressed as the spread continues. The eclectic nature of different online programs offered, from online degree programs, graduate programs, continuing studies, non-degree online courses, individual classes, certificates, and MOOCs, has risen from the individual needs of the school, degree program, or department that they are created to serve. With this comes a particularly staunch diversity, or perhaps incoordination, among different programs. This makes it difficult for different programs to share resources and knowledge. We need to think about distance education through a strategic institutional lens, and coordinate and centralize institutional efforts among different departments.

Quality control is another concern. Many of the preeminent, and often factually-incorrect issues stated with online education involve it being "easier", a predisposition to academic dishonestly, and instructors putting their online courses on the back-burner against their resident classes. While many of these issues are clearly present and accounted for in brick-and-mortar institutions, online education is the new kid on the block and has the opportunity to fix many of these problems. The Respondus Lockdown Browser, video tutoring, and online office hours are several of the efforts put forth by Arizona State to address these concerns, and I believe that continuing down the path of accountability, problem-solving, and long-term goal orientation will allow for ASU as well as many other online degree programs to flourish.

The future of online learning is bright. As our culture, both in academia and in the professional realm, begin to embrace it and accept it on the same level as an on-campus degree, I believe that distance education will allow more people than ever before to become educated and increase their quality of life. The evidence detailing self-determination and the educational value of online learning shows that it is often just as good, if not better than brick-and-mortar university education in the most important categories. As our culture continues to embrace online learning, in like fashion we can embrace this gilded age of learning with open arms, starry eyes, and bushy tails.

WORKS CITED PAGE

"2018 List of Accredited Online Colleges & Universities." *2018 Accredited Online Colleges & Universities*, GradReports, 12 Feb. 2018, www.guidetoonlineschools.com/online-schools.

Acemoglu, Daron, et al. "Equalizing Superstars: The Internet and the Democratization of Education." *SSRN*, University of Chicago , 22 Jan. 2014, papers.ssrn.com/sol3/papers.cfm?abstract_id=2382890.

Barbara|Toyama, et al. "Evaluation of Evidence-Based Practices in Online Learning: A Meta-Analysis and Review of Online Learning Studies." *US Department of Education*, US Department of Education. Available from: ED Pubs. P.O. Box 1398, Jessup, MD 20794-1398. Tel: 877-433-7827; Fax: 301-470-1244; Web Site: Http://Www.edpubs.org, 30 Apr. 2009, eric.ed.gov/?id=ED505824.

Bennett, William J. "Opinion: Is Sebastian Thrun's Udacity the Future of Higher Education?" *CNN*, Cable News Network, 5 July 2012, www.cnn.com/2012/07/05/opinion/bennett-udacity-education/index.html?no-st=1524937348.

Carr, Nicholas. "The Crisis in Higher Education." *MIT Technology Review*, MIT Technology Review, 11 Feb. 2016, www.technologyreview.com/s/429376/the-crisis-in-higher-education/.

Kim, Joshua. "Looking at the Future of Online Education Through a Strategic Institutional Lens | Inside Higher Ed." *Technology and Learning*, 19 Feb. 2018, www.insidehighered.com/blogs/technology-and-learning/looking-future-online-education-through-strategic-institutional-lens.

Kolowich, Steve. "Faculty Backlash Grows Against Online Partnerships." *The Chronicle of Higher Education*, The Chronicle of Higher Education, 6 May 2013, www.chronicle.com/article/faculty-backlash-grows-against/139049.

Marianne, et al. "Understanding the Implications of Online Learning for Educational Productivity." *Office of Educational Technology, US Department of Education*, Office of Educational Technology, US Department of Education. Available from: ED Pubs. P.O. Box 1398, Jessup, MD 20794-1398. Tel: 202-401-1444; Fax: 202-401-3941; Web Site: Http://www2.Ed.gov/about/Offices/List/Os/Technology/Index.html, 31 Dec. 2011, eric.ed.gov/?id=ED532492.

Selingo, Jeffrey. "The Future of College Looks Like the Future of Retail." *The Atlantic*, Atlantic Media Company, 16 Apr. 2018, www.theatlantic.com/education/archive/2018/04/college-online-degree-blended-learning/557642/.

Weigel, Margaret. "MOOCs and Online Learning: Research Roundup." *Journalist's Resource*, Harvard University, 24 May 2016, journalistsresource.org/studies/society/education/moocs-online-learning-research-roundup.

YOUR KNOWLEDGE HAS VALUE

- We will publish your bachelor's and master's thesis, essays and papers

- Your own eBook and book - sold worldwide in all relevant shops

- Earn money with each sale

Upload your text at www.GRIN.com
and publish for free